A GIFT FOR:

....

FROM:

....

This Christmas Night

Reflections from
Our Hearts to Your Home

Billy & Ruth Graham

Published by
THOMAS NELSON™
Since 1798
www.thomasnelson.com

CONTENTS

A NIGHT OF GREAT JOY

A NIGHT OF GLORIOUS GIFTS

A NIGHT OF EVERLASTING LOVE

 hristmas is the most thrilling season of the year. As we look back over the years, memories of many Christmases flood our minds. Christmas cards that we read and reread, the smell of pine drifting through the house, the fireplace crackling—all of these things turn our thoughts to those we love.

Ruth and I have treasured these moments spent with family and friends each year as we gather to celebrate the Christmas message: a message of hope and joy and love.

No other day on the calendar catches the imagination of young and old alike as does Christmas. It's a high and holy day—a day when the veil is drawn back and we get a fresh view of eternity.

It's a day when our minds go back to that lowly manger in Bethlehem, and we hear beyond the noise of our materialistic world the soft flutter of angels' wings. We see the tenderness of a mother with her first-born Son . . . we feel the softness of a Baby.

Christmas means something far deeper than human good will. It is the loving remembrance of the birth of the Savior. Over two thousand years ago, on a night the world has come to call Christmas, a young Jewish maiden went through the experience countless mothers had before her, and would since: She brought forth a child. But this was no ordinary child. This was the unique Son of God, sent from Heaven to save us from our sins (Matthew 2:11).

Christmas . . . it's the day we celebrate the birth of Jesus Christ, our Savior. Amid the glitter and busyness of the season, may you not lose sight of the miracle and meaning of that Christmas night. With the shepherds and the wise men, let us fall down and worship Him!

—BILLY AND RUTH GRAHAM

IN MEMORIAM, RUTH BELL GRAHAM, JUNE 10, 1920 – JUNE 14, 2007

This
Christmas Night

A Night of
Heavenly Hope

*Christmas is the most
significant of all the days
of the year.*

hristmas is not just a date on the calendar. It is the celebration of the event that set heaven to singing, an event that gave the stars of the night sky a new brilliance.

Eight hundred years before the birth of Christ, the prophet Isaiah declared: "The people who walked in darkness have seen a great light" (Isaiah 9:2). It was the promise of the coming of Christ and the light that was to dawn upon the world. It heralds the entrance of God into human history. It is heaven descending to earth. It is as though a trumpeter had taken his stand upon the turrets of time and announced to a despairing, hopeless, and frustrated world the coming of the Prince of Peace.

The Hebrew prophets not only believed in God but they worshiped God. They believed that God could be seen in nature. They believed that He had made the world. But all through the centuries they seem to have been saying, "I wish that God would become personal."

This is precisely what He did that first Christmas night. He became personal in Bethlehem. "The Word was made flesh, and dwelt among us" (John 1:14). At a specific time and at a specific place a specific person was born and that Person was God of very God, the Lord Jesus Christ.

From the lips of Jesus came these words, "The Son of man is come to seek and to save that which was lost" (Luke 19:10). Like piercing trumpets these words herald the breaking in of the Divine into human history. What a wonderful and glorious hope we have because of that first Christmas!

—DECISION, December 1985, "The Event that Set Heaven Singing"

O little town of Bethlehem,
How still we see thee lie!
Above thy deep and dreamless sleep
The silent stars go by.
Yet in thy dark streets shineth
The everlasting Light;
The hopes and fears of all the years
Are met in thee tonight.

For Christ is born of Mary,
And gathered all above,
While mortals sleep, the angels keep
Their watch of wondering love.
O morning stars together,
Proclaim the holy birth,
And praises sing to God the King,
And peace to men on earth!

How silently, how silently,
The wondrous gift is given;
So God imparts to human hearts
The blessings of His Heaven.
No ear may hear His coming,
But in this world of sin,
Where meek souls will receive Him still,
The dear Christ enters in.

O holy Child of Bethlehem,
Descend to us, we pray!
Cast out our sin and enter in,
Be born in us today.
We hear the Christmas angels,
The great glad tidings tell;
O come to us, abide with us,
Our Lord Emmanuel!

—BISHOP PHILLIPS BROOKS, 1868

And it came to pass in those days that a decree went out from Caesar Augustus that all the world should be registered. This census first took place while Quirinius was governing Syria. So all went to be registered, everyone to his own city.

Joseph also went up from Galilee, out of the city of Nazareth, into Judea, to the city of David, which is called Bethlehem, because he was of the house and lineage of David, to be registered with Mary, his betrothed wife, who was with child. So it was, that while they were there, the days were completed for her to be delivered. And she brought forth her firstborn Son, and wrapped Him in swaddling cloths, and laid Him in a manger, because there was no room for them in the inn.

—LUKE 2:1–7, NKJV

t had to be a very special time—the time when God's Son came into the world. God had chosen the children of Israel to build a nation for His Son, and the town of Bethlehem as His birthplace. But the Baby still had no family to care for Him. God was His father, but the Baby needed a mother.

God searched among His people for a woman worthy to be the mother of His Son. Would she be a princess living in a palace: or a rich man's daughter who wore bright dresses and jewels and had maids to arrange her hair and rub it with sweet-smelling perfume? God did not choose one of these. He chose instead a modest young girl named Mary, who lived in the little hill town of Nazareth in Galilee. He sent His angel Gabriel to tell Mary that she had been chosen to be the mother of His Son.

At first, Mary was so amazed that she could hardly speak. But she had always loved God and tried to obey Him. And so she said to the angel, *"I am the Lord's servant, and I am willing to do whatever he wants. May everything you said come true."*

She was going to marry a kind, strong man called Joseph. Long ago a man named Jeremiah had told the children of Israel that the Savior, when He came, would belong to the family of David, and both Mary and Joseph were members of that family, descended from the great King David. Joseph took good care of Mary as the time grew near for her Baby to be born. *(continued on page 31)*

(continued on page 31)

—Our Christmas Story

MARY

One evening in Jerusalem I looked out my hotel window and saw the lights of Bethlehem in the distance. For a long time I stood there and meditated on the events that had taken place over 2,000 years ago and which have transformed and changed our world.

I thought about the angel Gabriel. He came to Mary, who was no more than a teenager, and said, "Fear not, Mary; for thou hast found favor with God. And, behold, thou shalt conceive in thy womb, and bring forth a son, and shalt call his name Jesus. He shall be great, and shall be called the Son of the Highest; and the Lord God shall give unto him the throne of his father David: And he shall reign over the house of Jacob for ever: and of his kingdom there shall be no end" (Luke 1:30–33).

At first Mary was fearful and deeply disturbed. She asked the angel, "How shall this be, seeing I know not a man? And the angel answered and said unto her, The Holy Ghost shall come upon thee, and the power of the Highest shall overshadow thee; therefore also that holy thing which shall be born of thee shall be called the Son of God" (Luke 1:34–35).

Then Mary showed one of the most remarkable demonstrations of faith found in the Bible. Here she was, a virgin, engaged to a godly man by the name of Joseph, yet she was to be made pregnant supernaturally by the Holy Spirit. People would talk, shame could be attached to it, and Joseph might even reject her. But Mary by faith said, "Behold the handmaid of the Lord; be it unto me according to thy word" (Luke 1:38).

I believe that one of the greatest demonstrations of faith in all the Bible was Mary's answer to the angel in accepting God's will for her life, no matter what the cost.

—DECISION, December 1986, "Responses to the Christ Child"

*Christmas
is a time of miracles.
The angelic chorus,
lowly shepherds,
a humble manger as the
birthplace of deity—
all are miraculous
happenings.*

—Kenneth W. Osbeck

he emperor in Rome at that time was Caesar Augustus. Everybody in the world obeyed the emperor. But how many people was "everybody in the world"? Caesar didn't know.

So he decided to count them. Of course, he didn't want to count them just so that he could say, "Well, well. I am emperor of twenty million" (or however many it was). He wanted to know how many people he ruled so that he would know how much gold they could pay to him in taxes. In order to know how much each country should pay, Caesar had to count all the people in the world.

Now, in order to keep the different families and places in the huge empire straight, Caesar decided that everyone should go back to the town where his family had first lived, to be taxed there.

Now when Caesar Augustus decided something, it was the law. All over the Roman world people had to go to their hometowns and be counted for the tax. It might not be convenient to go. A farmer might be planting his wheat just then.

It might not even be safe. There might be old people in a family, or a very young baby, or perhaps a sick person. But when Caesar said, "Go!"—people went.

Nazareth, where Joseph and Mary lived, was almost a hundred miles from Bethlehem by the twisting road, and in those days a hundred miles was a tremendous distance. But they had no choice but to make the long journey. It was time for the Son of God to be born. *(continued on page 41)*

—Our Christmas Story

May the Christmas
morning make us happy to
be Thy children,
and the Christmas evening
bring us to our beds
with grateful thoughts,
forgiving and forgiven.

—Robert Louis Stevenson

hrist's birth was like no other in the history of the human race. For one thing, this Child had no human father. As the angel had promised Mary, "The Holy Spirit will come upon you, and the power of the Highest will overshadow you" (Luke 1:35).

In the Scriptures we are given just a little glimpse of Mary and Joseph before Jesus was born. They lived in the hill country of Galilee. Joseph was a religious man, and Mary gives every evidence of a thorough knowledge of the Scriptures, even though she was just a teenager.

Joseph was contracted to marry Mary, and in that time, being engaged was about the same as being married. I think we give too little attention to Joseph. He is called "a just man," (Matthew 1:19) which means he obeyed the will of God. It also includes the connotation of sympathy and kindness. It indicated his devotion to God and to Mary. The Greek word translated "husband" actually means "man." We are told that they had not come together as man and wife, that Mary and Joseph had kept their engagement love pure.

Then Mary was found to be with child. Put yourself in Joseph's place. Imagine his thoughts, his suspicions, about the girl to whom he was engaged. According to the ancient law, Mary should have been put to death. But Joseph did not want to have any part of that kind of punishment, so he decided to break the engagement privately.

While he was thinking about these things, God's angel appeared to him in a dream to give the prospective bridegroom an explanation of the situation. "Joseph, son of David," said the angel, "do not be afraid to take to you Mary your wife: for that which is conceived in her is of the Holy Spirit" (Matthew 1:20 NKJV).

When Joseph found that his wife-to-be was with child, he could have exposed her to the public. She might have been stoned. But he didn't because the angel had come to him in a dream, telling him, "Fear not! This Child that Mary will have is to be the Son of the Most High." What faith it took on Joseph's part to believe that message and to trust! He put away his suspicions. He believed God and was married to Mary. Like Mary, he said "Yes, Lord, regardless!"

—DECISION, 2001, "The Meaning of Christmas"; Decision, December 1968, "Good Tidings of Great Joy"

In this the love of God
was manifested toward us,
that God has sent His only
begotten Son into the world,
that we might live
through Him.

I John 4:9

O f all the times in the world to live, imagine being alive on the very day Jesus was born! What if we had lived not only at the very time but had been in the very town where Jesus was born! Families were coming to Bethlehem to pay taxes to an emperor they hated. They came in fear and anger. They didn't know, you see, that Christmas was about to happen.

Bethlehem was so crowded with travelers then that it must have been hard to move through the streets. Men tugged and shouted at heavy-laden donkeys, women carried tiny children, and older children lugged bundles of food. The people in the streets looked cross and tired. Some of them were headed for the large house where the Roman soldiers were taking names for the tax rolls. Others had just arrived in Bethlehem and were peering anxiously into the crowded doorways, wondering where they would find a place to spend the night. All they needed was room enough to spread out their cloaks and a little water to wash the dust of travel from their feet, but even those simple things were hard to find. Bethlehem had only one small inn and that had been filled by the first travelers to arrive, so the rest had to find a place to sleep in the houses of strangers, or in stables, or wherever there was room to lie down.

Suppose you had sat on the low stone wall near the gate where the north road came into Bethlehem to watch the latest strangers coming into town. Here came a whole family: four children, the mother and father, the grandmother, and that very old woman on the donkey must be the great-grandmother. They looked tired as they trudged up this last hill.

Alone and in groups the people came, walking rapidly on this last bit of their journey, up the hill to Bethlehem. Some of them, the old men said, were coming from as far away as the town of Nazareth. You could hardly believe it. Almost a hundred miles! That meant three or four nights of sleeping beside the road.

The afternoon sun was hot on your back. The wall was warm. For a minute, your eyes closed. When they opened, two people were coming along the dusty road down in the valley, a man walking and a woman riding a donkey. But how slowly these two were coming. The woman had her hand on the man's shoulder and she seemed very weary. The man kept looking at her anxiously.

Two men walking rapidly with tall staffs passed the couple and the donkey, climbed the hills, and went in through the town gate. Now the man and woman had reached the hill and you could see the donkey was covered with dust, as if he had come a long way. Why were they stopping so often, now that their trip was almost over? They stopped again, right in front of you. The woman turned to look at the man and as she did you saw her face. You saw it and your heart gave a little leap.

For on this young woman's face, so pale and travel-weary, was a smile that made you forget taxes and Roman soldiers and even Caesar Augustus himself. In hot, noisy, crowded Bethlehem, her smile seemed to say that all the joy of heaven had come down to earth.

That night, wrapped up in your cloak on the crowded floor of your house, you could not get to sleep for thinking of her smile. It was an unusual thing, these days, to see a happy face. You wondered if the man and woman had found a place to sleep. *(continued on page 59)*

—OUR CHRISTMAS STORY

I want to tell you about a man who was so caught up in his own problems that he missed the opportunity to be part of one of the greatest events of all times. This man actually missed Christmas altogether.

The Bible doesn't tell us the name of this man, but we can read his story in Luke 2:7:

[Mary] brought forth her firstborn son, . . .

and laid him in a manger;

because there was no room for them in the inn.

The One who brought Christmas, the One who gave us Christmas and who is Christmas could not find a room to be born in.

What was the cause of this tragedy? Why was there no room for Mary and Joseph and their expected Baby, except in a stable? Bethlehem was a small town, and in those days most small towns perhaps had only one inn. The inn in Bethlehem was already filled. No other accommodation was available.

I have some sympathy for the innkeeper, except in the matter of his preoccupation. He was not hostile; he was not opposed to the couple; but his inn was crowded; his hands were full; his mind was preoccupied.

The innkeeper was probably too taken up with his duties to be bothered with a carpenter from Nazareth and his expectant wife. After all, it was an unusually busy time, with guests arriving from every corner of Israel for the census and taxation. It was a time for renewing of acquaintances, for conviviality, and for bringing in the cash receipts. There was no time for idle sentiments. The innkeeper could not be disturbed by a young expectant mother.

He probably told Joseph, "I wish I could help you, but I must keep my priorities. After all, this is a business, and this coming Child is no real concern of mine. But I'm not a hardhearted man. Over there is the stable. You are welcome to use it if you care to, but that is the best I can do. Now I must get back to my work. My guests need me."

He was too busy to notice a woman about to give birth to a Baby, to a Child who would grow up to become the most famous Man in all of history, and more than a Man, the Son of God, the Messiah, the Prince of Peace.

No room for Jesus? No room for the King of kings? This is the answer that millions are giving today. It is the answer of preoccupation—not fierce opposition, not furious hatred, but unconcern about spiritual things.

Things have not really changed since that Bethlehem night two thousand years ago. God is still on the fringes of most of our lives. We fit Him in when it is convenient for us, but we become irritated when He makes demands on us. Our lives are so full. There is so much to be done. But in all our busy activities are we in danger of excluding from our hearts and lives the One who made us?

—DECISION, December 2000, "Are You Going to Miss Christmas?"

There was
no room for Jesus
in the world that
He had made—
imagine!

mong the most tragic words ever penned are those found in Luke's account of the first Christmas. "There was no room for them in the inn." There was room for merchants, tax collectors, travelers and sightseers, but no room for the gentle Mary and the divine Christ, who was to be born that night.

An event that was destined to stir and shape the universe caused little excitement in a world that was drugged with selfishness and numbed by greed. The Roman legions certainly were not interested in the advent of a tiny babe, born in a humble stable. The priests were too preoccupied with their legalistic sacrifices and ceremonies to see in him the fulfillment of all that God had promised through the centuries. The mercenary merchant was too busy plying his wares, driving hard and profitable bargains, to turn aside and see him who was the hope of the world. What a picture of the inhospitality and indifference of the human heart. No room for the Son of God.

Mary, the young mother of the Son of God, did not have the loving care provided for most women in such circumstances. She had to be her own maid and midwife. There was no spotless sheet on which to lay her firstborn; only the straw of the manger. There were no nurses in skilful attendance; no doctors coming and going, whispering counsel to each other. There was only the lowing of the cattle and the soft breathing of the child Jesus. There was not even a cot on which to lay Him.

Earthly princes make their entrance into the world amid the comforts of lavish splendor, while their subjects await with bated breath the announcement that a prince has been born. But when Christ the Son of God came into the world only a few humble shepherds and some Magi from the East were aware that a king had been born. He whose name is above every name, He who is the Prince of Peace and the Prince of Heaven, was wrapped in simple rags and laid in a manger because there was no room for them in the inn.

Today, after two thousand years of Christianity, there is still danger that we will be too busy this season to make room for Christ. Billions of dollars are being spent by Christmas shoppers. The stores are filled with people rushing here and there, absorbed with the business of buying gifts. People flock to holiday parties, to programs, to bazaars, to special banquets; but now, as then, there is danger that we will be too busy to make room for Him.

This Christ who came as a babe in Bethlehem to die on the cross and to rise from the grave, can transform and change your life, no matter what your circumstances may be—if there is room in your heart for Him.

—DECISION, December 1962, "No Room in the Inn"

A Night
of Wonder

*Christmas represents a hope,
a unique joy,
felt only at Christmastime,
because Christ the Savior
is born.*

magine the scene in Bethlehem. It was the night of nights, and yet it had begun as every other night had before it. Toward the west was the Mediterranean Sea, and the sun was beginning to sink until across the western sky was a great bar of gold.

As the sky turned gray, and after that the night, one could look to the east and make out the mountains of Moab rising out of the shadows like colossal giants. In Bethlehem's houses mothers lay their children down to sleep. In the courtyards of the inn some camels lay down to rest. Here and there in homes lamps gleamed for a moment, then went out. In the fields the sheep lay down while the shepherds sat near their fires.

In the heavens above appeared the same stars that had shined throughout all the ages, ever since God had made the stars to rule by night.

Yes, it was night. But it was to become the greatest, most significant night of history. This was the night that would conquer darkness and bring in the day when there would be night no more. This was the night when they who sat in darkness would see a great light. This was the night that God brought into the world the One who is "the light of the world" (John 8:12). What a moment! What an hour!

—DECISION, December 1988, "Immanuel! God with Us!";
Decision, December 1971, "The Night of Nights"

Now there were in the same country shepherds living out in the fields, keeping watch over their flock by night. And behold, an angel of the Lord stood before them, and the glory of the Lord shone around them, and they were greatly afraid. Then the angel said to them, "Do not be afraid, for behold, I bring you good tidings of great joy which will be to all people. For there is born to you this day in the city of David a Savior, who is Christ the Lord. And this will be the sign to you: You will find a Babe wrapped in swaddling cloths, lying in a manger."

And suddenly there was with the angel a multitude of the heavenly host praising God and saying: "Glory to God in the highest, and on earth peace, goodwill toward men!"

—LUKE 2:8–14, NKJV

Christmas is
not a myth,
not a tradition,
not a dream—it is
a glorious reality.

L et's imagine once again what it might have been like to be living in Bethlehem that night. Wrapped in your cloak on the crowded floor of your house, you could not get to sleep for thinking of the woman on the donkey and her lovely smile. Why was she so happy? And you, why were you so wide-awake and excited tonight?

This was a special night. You didn't know how you knew it, but you knew that something wonderful was about to happen to you— to you and to everyone. Something so wonderful you were almost afraid to breathe for fear of breaking the stillness.

For tonight Bethlehem was very still. On other nights donkeys coughed in their stables and wolves howled from their hill tops. But on this most special of all nights, even the donkeys and the wolves were quiet. The wind itself stopped blowing. The animals and the sky and a few wide-awake children were quiet. Listening. Waiting for something.

It was very late in the night when you suddenly jumped up from the floor. There was a commotion out in the street. You could hear men shouting, running, their sandals scuffing on the rough stones of the street. You ran to the door and stared at these men who were talking so loudly in the middle of the night. They looked like country men, sheepherders. What was it they were saying? They had seen an angel!

You looked at them again to make sure they were really shepherds and not lunatics. No, they were tough-looking surely, but not crazy—strong men who lived out of doors and fought wolves from their sheep with nothing but a few sticks and stones. They were not the kind of men who would be imagining things.

They had seen an angel, they repeated. And the angel had told them about a Baby born in Bethlehem and called the Baby "Savior" and "Lord." They had just seen the Baby with their own eyes—out in the stable behind the inn—and they wanted everyone else to know about it, too.

You didn't wait to hear any more. You set off down the street as fast as you could run, past houses where sleepy people were stumbling to the doors, asking what all the racket was about. To the inn, then around it to the stable, then, slowly, softly, in at the door.

There she was. The young woman with the radiant smile. She was leaning against one of the stalls, and the eyes in her happy face were closed. The man was at her side. And behind them, in the manger where the cows came for their food, was the Baby.

He was a tiny thing, wrapped tightly in a long linen band of cloth and sleeping soundly as any newborn baby. Sleeping as though the world had not waited thousands of years for this moment. As soundly as though your life and my life and the life of everyone on earth were not wrapped up in His birth.

Should you speak to His mother resting so quietly there? Should you ask her if you might touch the Baby—not to wake Him, but just to touch His hand?

What a moment that would have been! To have reached out your own hand and touched the Son of God!

—Our Christmas Story

Away in a manger,
no crib for a bed,
the little Lord Jesus
laid down His sweet head;
the stars in the sky
looked down where He lay,
the little Lord Jesus,
asleep on the hay.

The cattle are lowing;
the Baby awakes,
but little Lord Jesus,
no crying He makes;
I love Thee, Lord Jesus!
look down from the sky,
and stay by my cradle
till morning is nigh.

Be near me, Lord Jesus,

I ask Thee to stay

close by me forever,

and love me, I pray;

bless all the dear children

in Thy tender care,

and fit us for heaven,

to live with Thee there.

—John Thomas McFarland, 1851–1913

 t is God's way to begin small. When He decided to redeem and save a world, it might be expected that He would rend the heavens and astonish the world with the terror of His majesty and the beauty of His love. But He did not. He started with a baby in a cow stable. He could scarcely have made a smaller beginning.

Here in the dark cave, as a flickering torch casts high shadows of long-horned oxen on the rough-hewn logs, there is no sound but the munching of hay by the cattle. In the midst lies the young mother, forgetting for the moment her discomfort, for in her arms lies the Babe, her baby boy. About His face still plays the light of heaven from which He came. Its unclouded purity still lingers in His eyes. Who would dream that He is the King of kings and Lord of lords? Who would imagine in Bethlehem that night that He would reach down the ages, overturning kingdoms and empires, changing the world.

Cradled in the manger in Bethlehem were the hopes and dreams of a dying world. Those chubby little hands that clasped the straw in His manger crib were soon to open blinded eyes, unstop deaf ears, and still the troubled seas. That cooing voice was soon to be lifted to command demons to depart, to teach men of the Way, and to raise the dead. Those tiny feet were to take Him to the sick and needy and were finally to be pierced on Calvary's Cross.

That manger crib in remote Bethlehem became the link that bound a lost world to a loving God. Christmas is not a myth, not a tradition, not a dream—it is a glorious reality. From that manger came a Man who not only taught us a new way of life, but brought us into a new relationship with our Creator.

—Decision, December 1971, "The Night of Nights"

She will bring
forth a Son,
and you shall call
His name Jesus,
for He will save
His people
from their sins."

—Matthew 1:21 NKJV

A Mother's Prayer

Had I been Joseph's mother
I'd have prayed
protection from his brothers:
"God keep him safe;
he is so young,
so different from
the others."
Mercifully she never knew
there would be slavery
and prison, too.

Had I been Moses' mother
I'd have wept
to keep my little son;
praying she might forget
the babe drawn from the water
of the Nile,
had I not kept
him for her
nursing him the while?

Was he not mine
and she
but Pharaoh's daughter? . . .

Had I been Mary—
Oh, had I been she,
I would have cried
as never a mother cried,
". . . Anything, O God,
anything . . .
but crucified!"

With such prayers
importunate
my finite wisdom
would assail
Infinite Wisdom;
God, how fortunate
Infinite Wisdom
should prevail!

—Ruth Bell Graham's Collected Poems

We also rejoice in God
through our Lord Jesus Christ,
through whom we have
now received the
reconciliation.

Romans 5:11

**O**ver 2,000 years ago, on a night the world has been pleased to call "Christmas," a Jewish maiden went to the mysterious depths of motherhood and came back with a Child. This Child was given a name—

A Name

that blossoms on the pages of history
like the flowers of a thousand springtimes;

A Name

that echoes down the corridors of time like the music
of a thousand choirs in one grand anthem;

A Name

that adorns the records of the centuries like the splendor of a thousand
monuments built of the purest and most precious stones;

A Name

that after 2,000 years of scrutiny shines in the galaxy of earth's great souls
like the glory of a thousand suns;

A Name

that is greater, grander, more glorious and more meaningful
than all the names of the world put together.

On December 25 the birthday of Jesus Christ will be celebrated all over the world. It will be celebrated in various ways, in many languages, by people of all races. For a few hours many in the world will stop talking of satellites, rockets, and war. For a few hours many will talk of peace on earth and good will toward men. People will exchange their gifts and talk about the Prince of Peace.

—Decision, December 1987, "Christ, the Center of Christmas"

Christmas tells us
that at a specific time
and place
a specific Person was born.
That Person was
God of very God,
the Lord Jesus Christ.

Unto us a Child is born,
Unto us a Son is given;
And the government will be
upon His shoulder.
And His name
will be called Wonderful,
Counselor, Mighty God,
Everlasting Father,
Prince of Peace.

—Isaiah 9:6 nkjv

ive awe-inspiring names of our Lord Jesus encourage us, thrill us, and fill us with hope at this Christmas season.

1. JESUS IS CALLED WONDERFUL. He was wonderful in His life. He mingled with sinners, yet was sinless. He associated with publicans and sinners but never partook of their sins. His enemies could find not one flaw in His character; He was without reproach.

Jesus was also wonderful in His death, the fitting climax to His selfless living. He lived for others; He died for others.

2. JESUS IS CALLED COUNSELOR. If ever the world needed the counsel of Christ, it does today. Thousands of people everywhere in this world who have accepted Christ, the Divine Advocate, have found the Solution to their baffling problems.

3. JESUS IS CALLED THE MIGHTY GOD. When the wrongs of the world needed righting and a fallen race needed redemption, God did not send His heavenly

angelic armies to accomplish His majestic purpose; He sent a tiny, tender, helpless Babe in the Person of His Son. Jesus is the God-Man.

4. JESUS IS CALLED THE EVERLASTING FATHER. He had no beginning and He has no end. When Jesus was born of a virgin, that was not His beginning, it was His incarnation. He is the designer of the entire universe. "Before Abraham was, I am," He said (John 8:58).

5. JESUS IS CALLED THE PRINCE OF PEACE. We cannot have peace in our hearts apart from our relationship with Jesus Christ. He will give His peace to us this Christmas if we put our trust and our faith in Him.

—DECISION, December, 1989, "When God's Son Came to Earth";
Decision, December 1998, "The Message of Christmas"

SILENT NIGHT, HOLY NIGHT

Silent Night! Holy Night!

All is calm, all is bright.
Round yon virgin mother and child!
Holy Infant so tender and mild,
sleep in heavenly peace, sleep in heavenly peace!

Silent night! Holy night!
Shepherds quake at the sight;
glories stream from heaven afar;
heav'nly hosts sing alleluia—
Christ the Savior is born! Christ the Savior is born!

Silent night! Holy night!
Son of God, love's pure light
radiant beams from Thy holy face
with the dawn of redeeming grace—

Jesus, Lord at Thy birth, Jesus, Lord at Thy birth.

—Joseph Mohr, 1818

A tiny secluded manger with its sweet-smelling straw and its lowing cattle comprised the homely stage upon which the most striking and significant drama of the centuries was enacted. It was there that God, in the Person of His Son, Jesus Christ, became identified with man. In meekness and humility He came to earth as the Prince of Peace.

During the First World War, on Christmas Eve, the battlefield was strangely quiet. As the soft snow fell, the thoughts of the young men were of home and their families. Softly one lad began to hum "Silent Night." Wheezy tenors and throaty baritones took up the chorus until the trenches resounded with the Christmas song. When they finished singing, they were astonished to hear the song echoing from the trenches across no-man's-land: In their own tongue the other soldiers also sang "Silent Night." That night they were thinking of the Prince of Peace, the Christ of Christmas.

How different this world would be if we could unite together around that "Holy Infant so tender and mild." Earth can be as Heaven with Christ. Discord can be as peace when Christ is near. Midnight gloom can be transformed into noonday

brightness when He abides with us.

—DECISION, December, 1989, "When God's Son Came to Earth"

*Christmas
is a reminder from
God Himself that we
are not alone.*

hrist came into a world that had problems much like the ones with which we grapple today. We often imagine that the world to which Jesus came was not complicated and that its problems were not complex. But historians tell us otherwise. They tell us that the problems of that day were similar to the problems of our day.

The world that Jesus came to was a deeply disturbed world. People faced the complexities of life with difficulty. They broke under the strain; they sought ways to escape the problems that perplexed them.

To those without the joy of living, Jesus said, "I am come that they might have life, and that they might have it more abundantly" (John 10:10).

To those who bore the chafing burden of the guilt of sin, he said, "Be of good cheer; your sins are forgiven" (Matthew 9:2 NKJV).

To the friendless he said, "I call you not servants; . . . but I have called you friends" (John 15:15).

Christmas means that Immanuel has come—that God is with us (Matthew 1:23).

It means that our sordid, failure-fraught pasts can be defeated and changed by Jesus' sacrifice on the cross and His victorious resurrection. It means that we can be brought into God's family, heirs of God and citizens of heaven. Christmas means that God comes into the night of our suffering and sorrow, saying, "I am with you always" and, "I will give you rest" (Matthew 28:20; 11:28).

My prayer is that the message of this Christmastime will be a personal message to you, that Jesus will be a Wonderful Savior to you, that He will be the Prince of Peace in your life, bringing peace, satisfaction, and joy.

—DECISION, December 2003, "Light for a Darkened World";
December 1980, "What Does Christmas Mean?"

LAY THEM AT HIS FEET

Lay them quietly at His feet one by one;
each desire, however sweet, just begun;
dreams still hazy, growing bright;
hope just poised, winged for flight;
all your longing, each delight—every one.

At His feet and leave them there,
never fear;
every heartache, crushing care—trembling tear;
you will find Him always true,
men may fail you, friends be few,
He will prove Himself to you
far more dear.

—RUTH BELL GRAHAM'S COLLECTED POEMS

A Night of Great Joy

The birth of the
Christ child in
Bethlehem was worthy
of the angels!

So it was, when the angels had gone away from them into heaven, that the shepherds said to one another, "Let us now go to Bethlehem and see this thing that has come to pass, which the Lord has made known to us." And they came with haste and found Mary and Joseph, and the Babe lying in a manger. Now when they had seen Him, they made widely known the saying which was told them concerning this Child. And all those who heard it marveled at those things which were told them by the shepherds. But Mary kept all these things and pondered them in her heart. Then the shepherds returned, glorifying and praising God for all the things that they had heard and seen, as it was told them.

—LUKE 2:15–20 NKJV

he first Christmas worship service was conducted not in a temple, or in a cathedral, or in a synagogue, but in the great out-of-doors. The stars stone like diamonds in the cold, crisp sky. On the hills outside the little village of Bethlehem the flocks had been gathered, and watch was being kept to protect them from the constant threat of roving wolves or marauding bandits. The little band of weary shepherds had followed the same routine for countless generations.

Like most of the people of Palestine, they were poor and insignificant men, from all outward appearances. They had no reason to expect that this night would be different from any other. But God had other plans. This was the night when God Himself would come to earth. The dull routine of their lives was suddenly and dramatically shattered by the appearance of an angel.

The tidings of Christ's birth echoed across the skies. The angel of the Lord proclaimed the good news to lowly shepherds. The shepherds, though poor, could discern the voice from heaven above the noisy din of earth's confusion. Strange that this glad word was not first given to the priests or the scholars or the Pharisees. God speaks to those who are prepared in their hearts to listen, and the shepherds of Judea heard this sermon from the skies.

The news brought by the angel of the Lord on that first Christmas night was the greatest news ever come to mankind. The news is good because fear has been replaced by hope, hatred by love, greed by unselfishness, bondage by freedom, guilt by pardon.

It is good news because the world has taken on a new look. Joy replaced sadness; fellowship replaced separation; our hearts are tilted up in hope rather than bowed down in despair.

It is good news because holy laughter rings once more throughout the earth. God's voice and the voices of men and women had not been blended in holy laughter since the days of their fellowship in the Garden of Eden. But once more, through Christ, the thrill of fellowship is experienced between God and man.

—DECISION, December 1990, "The Night an Angel Spoke"

Christ has
come to give us hope.
To give us a new song.
To heal our
spiritual wounds...
if we will let Him.

Angels we have heard on high,

sweetly singing o'er the plains,

and the mountains, in reply,

echoing their joyous strains.

Shepherds, why this jubilee?

Why your joyous strains prolong?

What the gladsome tidings be

which inspire your heav'nly song?

Come to Bethlehem and see

Him whose birth the angels sing;

come, adore on bended knee

Christ the Lord, the new-born King.

See Him in a manger laid,

Jesus, Lord of heav'n and earth;

Mary, Joseph, lend your aid,

with us sing our Savior's birth.

Refrain: Gloria in excelsis Deo!

—18TH CENTURY FRENCH CAROL

Those were no ordinary sheep . . .

no common flocks,

huddled in sleep

among the fields,

the layered rocks,

near Bethlehem

That Night;

but those

selected for the Temple sacrifice:

theirs to atone

for sins

they had not done.

How right

the angels should appear

to them

That Night.

Those were no usual shepherds there,
but outcast shepherds
whose unusual care
of special sheep
made it impossible to keep
Rabbinic law,
which therefore banned them.

How right
the angels should appear
to them
That Night.

—Ruth Bell Graham's Collected Poems

You, O Lord,
shall endure forever,
and the remembrance of
Your name to all
generations.

Psalm 102:12

Christmas means
something vastly deeper
than human good will.
It is the loving
remembrance of the birth
of the Savior.

THE ANGELS

he Bible does not tell us in detail about the angels of God, but it makes clear that they are the highest beings in God's created universe. So it is not strange that it was an angel, joined by a host of angels, who first announced the birth of the Messiah. No other event in history would touch the lives of so many people or affect so profoundly the course of human history. The birth of the Christ child in Bethlehem was worthy of the angels!

What is the message of the Christmas angels?

First of all, it is a message of love and peace. "Glory to God in the highest, and on earth peace, good will toward men" sang the angelic multitude (Luke 2:14). It is a message of joy and hope. "Behold, I bring you good tidings of great joy, which shall be to all people" (Luke 2:10). The message of the Christmas angels is that God not only exists, but that He is a loving heavenly Father who seeks to restore us to what we were created to be—His children. Because God's Son, Jesus Christ, has entered this world, we know beyond a shadow of doubt that joy and hope can be ours if we will but receive the gift of Christmas.

How fitting it was that God chose the glorious angels to bring the news to men of the birth of the Son of God.

—Decision, December 1976, "That Night Near Bethlehem"

WHILE SHEPHERDS WATCHED
THEIR FLOCKS BY NIGHT

Whilst Shepherds watched their flocks by night,
All seated on the ground,
The Angel of the Lord came down,
And glory shone around.

"Fear not," said he, for mighty dread
Had seized their troubled mind,
"Glad tidings of great joy I bring
To you and all mankind."

"To you in David's town this day
Is born of David's line
A Saviour, who is Christ the Lord,
And this shall be the sign."

"The heav'nly Babe you there shall find,
To human view display'd,
All meanly wrapp't in swaddling bands,
And in a manger laid."

Thus spake the Seraph, and forthwith
Appeared a shining throng
Of Angels, praising God, who thus
Addressed their joyful song:

"All glory be to God on high,
And to the earth be peace;
Good will henceforth from Heav'n to men
Begin and never cease."

—DAVIES GILBERT, 1822

hat was the content of the sermon of the angel on that first Christmas night? "Fear not" (Luke 2:10). Before Christ came, the world was filled with fear. The Romans feared rebellion, and their subjects feared Rome's power. The Sadducees feared the Pharisees, and they both were suspect of the publicans. The hearts of people everywhere were filled with suspicion, fear, and distrust.

Four times in the Gospel accounts of Christmas the angels used the expression, "Fear not."

Zacharias, an old man, was filled with fear when an angel appeared. He was told that he would be a father and that his son would be the forerunner of the Messiah. The angel told him, "Fear not" (Luke 1:13).

Mary was told that she would have the awesome privilege of bearing the Son of God. Fear filled her at first, but the angel said, "Fear not, Mary" (Luke 1:30).

Joseph, betrothed to Mary, was filled with fear and embarrassment when he learned that she was pregnant. But the angel declared, "Fear not . . ." (Matthew 1:20).

Then when the Holy Child was born, the angel came to those shepherds in the fields and said, "Fear not: for, behold I bring you good tidings of great joy" (Luke 2:10).

And that is what God says to us today, no matter what our fears may be. He is saying to you right now "Fear not." Why? Because Christ is with us. Jesus declared, "In the world ye shall have tribulation; but be of good cheer; I have overcome the world" (John 16:33). He invites you to bring your cares and your burdens to Him.

—DECISION, December 1984, "The Peace of Christmas"

Christ
shared in our humanity
so we could share in
His divinity.

GOD'S GREAT LOVE

I heard of one mother who every day showed her young son a large portrait of his father who was away at war. One day the young boy looked long and wistfully at his father's picture and said, "Mom, wouldn't it be great if Dad would just step down from the frame?"

For centuries people have looked into the heavens—longing for God to step out of the frame. In Bethlehem so many years ago God did exactly that. He stepped out of the frame.

The virgin-born Baby was God in human form. He took the form of a servant. He identified Himself with the problems of the entire human race.

Christmas tells us what it cost God to save the world: "For God so loved the world, that he gave his only begotten Son" (John 3:16). Christ is God's great Christmas Gift to the world. He does for us what no other has been able to do: He removes our guilt, reconciles us to God. He raises us from the death of sin to the life of righteousness. He implants within us new hopes, new aims, new enthusiasm.

When Christ comes into a life, He revolutionizes it so that the person becomes a "new creation" (2 Corinthians 5:17, RSV). This, and this alone, is our hope.

This hope that was given to those shepherds on that first Christmas morning is available only to those who believe. To know the pardon, joy, peace, and power that come through Christ, we must personally receive Him by faith. We must humble ourselves and admit our sin and our moral failure. And then by faith we must turn to Him as Savior and Lord.

From two momentous events, the birth and death of Jesus, God says to us, "I love you." He also says, "I can forgive you."

—DECISION, December 2002, "Unto You Is Born this Day";
Decision, December 2005, "You Can Know the Christ of Christmas"

The fact that
Jesus came is written in history.
It is written on the calendar.
It is written in the Bible.
It is written
on your conscience.

Like other shepherds

help me keep

watch over my flock by night;

mindful of each need,

each hurt, which might

lead one to stray,

each weakness

and each ill—

while others sleep

teach me to pray.

At night the wolves and leopards,

hungry and clever; prowl

in search of strays,

and wounded; when they howl,

Lord, still

my anxious heart

to calm delight—

for the Great Shepherd

watches with me

over my flock

by night.

—Ruth Bell Graham's Collected Poems

hristmas means different things to different people. To some, Christmas merely means an opportunity to make more money. Some people vie with each other in their preparations for the celebration. Pleasure-seeking consumes the time and thoughts of many people. Others are so busy with a thousand and one things to do that they have no time to even consider the message of the Baby of Bethlehem.

I am reminded of a story about the day that Abraham Lincoln was born in Kentucky. A neighbor hailed a man from town and said, "Any news down at the village, Ezra?"

"Well, Squire McLean's gone to Washington to see Madison sworn in, and old Spellman tells me that this Bonaparte fellow has captured most of Spain. What's new out here, neighbor?"

"Nothing at all, nothing at all, except a new baby down at Tom Lincoln's house. Nothing ever happens out here."

The birth of Abraham Lincoln, but it was not considered important! And the birth of Jesus Christ, but to many millions, the true meaning of Christmas is still unimportant. This is hard to comprehend when the good news of Christmas is still the same today as it was when the angels first announced it: "Unto you is born this day . . . a Savior" (Luke 2:11). Heaven and earth joined together! God and mankind reconciled. Hope for the hopeless, pardon for the guilty, forgiveness for the conscious-stricken, peace for those who knew no peace, good news for those who have had nothing but bad news.

Christmas is a reminder from God Himself that we are not alone. Jesus Christ is here. He is here to give us hope, to forgive our sins, to give us a new song, to impart faith, and to heal our spiritual wounds if only we will let Him.

—Decision, December 1993, "Christmas a Time of Renewed Hope"

hristmas should be a time of renewed hope—not hope in the status quo, not hope in a particular concept—but hope in Jesus Christ. Hope that God is still in the shadow of history, hope that despite our tangled bungling God will bring order out of chaos.

Today our imaginations go back two thousand years to that first Christmas when the world experienced three phenomena. First, there was a *star*. There were many stars in the sky, but none like this. This one shone with the aura and brilliance of another world. It was as though God had taken a lamp from the ceiling of heaven and hung it in the dark sky over a troubled world.

Second, there was a *new song* in the air. A world that had lost its song learned to sing again. With the coming of God in the flesh hope sprang in the heart of man; and led by angelic beings, the whole world took up the refrain, "Glory to God in the highest, and on earth peace, good will toward men" (Luke 2:14).

And third, there was *good news*—the good news that at last a Savior had come to save men from sin. He was the central theme of that first Christmas. The star, the song , the gifts, the joy, the hope, the excitement—all were because of Him.

—Decision, December 1969 "Christmas: God with Us"

GOD REST ME, PLEASE

"God rest you merry,
gentlemen . . ."
and in these pressured days
I, too, would seek to be so blessed
by Him, who still conveys
His merriment, along with rest.
So I would beg, on tired knees,
"God rest me merry,
please . . ."

—RUTH BELL GRAHAM'S COLLECTED POEMS

ere at the Graham home everything is ready for Christmas. The old log walls are fairly bulging with family and friends gathered for the occasion. The tree is trimmed and all alight, the boxwood wreath is hanging over the mantel, the beeswax candles are on the end table, the Yule log is on the back of the fire, and all the little things that help to emphasize the specialness of the season are here.

As we have been busy preparing, it has dawned on me that Christmas is a time not only for giving but for taking away. To make room for the Christmas tree, the rubber plant had to be taken away. To hang the wreath, the old blue platter on the mantel had to be taken away. To make room for the candles, favorite pieces of bric-a-brac had to be taken away. To accommodate the Yule log, the ashes had to be taken away. In honor of the occasion even the dust and cobwebs had to go!

So here is a special message from the Bible for us all this Christmas: "The LORD gives, and the LORD takes away; blessed be the name of the LORD" (See Job 1:21).

Since our lives are made better and happier not only by what God gives but by what He takes away, our prayer for us all this Christmas is that God will take away from our lives anything that may be keeping us from receiving Him, without whom any other gift is not worth receiving.

—RUTH
(*Decision*, December 1968, "The Quiet Corner")

*Christ came
into this world as
God's Ambassador,
sent from Heaven to tell us
of God's love.*

A Night of Glorious Gifts

The gift
He wants most
is your heart.

O nce again, at this sacred season of the year, the world comes under the magic spell of Christmas. Children step with a softer, more expectant tread, and with a light of hope and anticipation in their eyes. The bright holiday trappings are brought tenderly from their places of storage, and once more they deck the happy halls of home.

The familiar scent of pine and cedar pervades the atmosphere as Yule logs are piled high in preparation for the day of days. Holly and mistletoe are gathered from the hillside by the farmer, or are brought from the open-air market by the city-folk.

The air is filled with the sound of caroling, and a happy twinkle is found in the misty eyes of both young and old. Mother and Dad whisper secrets, and young ears listen intently for the tiniest hint of what is to come. Children peek through partly open doors to watch the careful wrapping of boxed gifts, beautifully tied by loving hands.

What is happening to the so-common boredom and melancholy of life? Whence comes this new zest, this anticipation, this gracious spirit of sharing? I'll tell you what it is: The world once more is cocking its ear to catch the accent of angel voices. The world once more is being illuminated by the light of the Christmas star.

Just as surely as those first shepherds heard the celestial music echoing over the countryside, and the Magi from the east discerned the strange new star that had swum into their universe, so thousands today by faith are hearing the distant melodies of heaven, and are beholding the Christmas star.

—DECISION, December 1964, "The Light of the Star"

Now after Jesus was born in Bethlehem of Judea in the days of Herod the king, behold, wise men from the East came to Jerusalem, saying, "Where is He who has been born King of the Jews? For we have seen His star in the East and have come to worship Him."

When Herod the king heard this, he was troubled, and all Jerusalem with him. And when he had gathered all the chief priests and scribes of the people together, he inquired of them where the Christ was to be born.

So they said to him, "In Bethlehem of Judea, for thus it is written by the prophet:

'But you, Bethlehem, in the land of Judah,

Are not the least among the rulers of Judah;

For out of you shall come a Ruler

Who will shepherd My people Israel.'"

(continued)

Then Herod, when he had secretly called the wise men, determined from them what time the star appeared. And he sent them to Bethlehem and said, "Go and search carefully for the young Child, and when you have found Him, bring back word to me, that I may come and worship Him also."

When they heard the king, they departed; and behold, the star which they had seen in the East went before them, till it came and stood over where the young Child was. When they saw the star, they rejoiced with exceedingly great joy. And when they had come into the house, they saw the young Child with Mary His mother, and fell down and worshiped Him. And when they had opened their treasures, they presented gifts to Him: gold, frankincense, and myrrh.

Then, being divinely warned in a dream that they should not return to Herod, they departed for their own country another way.

—MATTHEW 2:1–12 NKJV

On Christmas day, when our children were little, they would awaken before daylight, their eyes dancing with expectation to open the gifts. Before we opened the gifts, we read the Bible and prayed. What a thrill it was to celebrate the birthday of God's Son, Jesus Christ.

One of the passages that we read was from the Gospel of Matthew, where the wise men came from the East to Jerusalem, following a star. They came to the house of Joseph, fell down and worshiped the Christ Child, and "presented unto him gifts; gold, frankincense, and myrrh" (Matthew 2:11).

From His very birth Christ was recognized as King. Something about Him inspired allegiance, loyalty and homage. Wise men brought Him gifts. Shepherds fell down and worshiped Him. Herod, realizing that there is never room for two thrones in one kingdom, sought Jesus' life.

As Jesus began His ministry, His claims upon people's lives were total and absolute. He allowed no divided loyalty. He demanded and received complete adoration and devotion. Mature men and women left their businesses and gave themselves in complete obedience to Him. Many of them gave their lives, pouring out the last full measure of devotion.

His words caused even His most avowed enemies to say, "Never man spake like this Man" (John 7:46). And yet He was more than a poet, more than a statesman, more than a physician. We cannot understand Christ until we understand that He was the King of kings and the Lord of lords. Like Thomas, our only response must be to bow down and confess, "My Lord and my God!" (John 20:28).

The wise men of old inquired, "Where is he that is born King?" (Matthew 2:2) The Bible says of Him: "Jesus Christ the same yesterday, and today, and forever" (Hebrews 13:8). He was King yesterday, He is King today, He will be King tomorrow.

Every year people write me saying how much they dread Christmas. Often their complaint stems from how busy they will be, or how much money they will spend.

Did those wise men who journeyed hundreds of miles across the desert to seek out the infant Jesus ever feel that way? After all, it took months to make the arduous trip, and they had gone to great expense to provide gifts of gold, frankincense, and myrrh for the new child.

I doubt it. In fact, as their journey neared its end we read they had "exceedingly great joy." What made the difference? Their focus was totally on Jesus, the One who would be called "Immanuel . . . God with us" (Matthew 1:23).

Don't let this Christmas season overwhelm you. Don't feel you have to do everything, or go into debt just to impress other people. Focus instead on Jesus. Take time every day to read the prophecies of His coming, and the wonderful story of His birth. Make this Christmas one of "exceedingly great joy"!

—DECISION, December 1999, "The Baby, the King";
Decision, December 1992, "The King Is Born"

Holy, holy, holy
is the LORD of hosts;
The whole earth is full of
His glory!

Isaiah 6:3

WE THREE KINGS

We three kings of Orient are,

bearing gifts we traverse afar,

field and fountain, moor and mountain,

following yonder star.

Chorus

O star of wonder, star of night,

Star with royal beauty bright,

Westward leading, still proceeding,

Guide us to Thy perfect light.

Born a King on Bethlehem's plain,

gold I bring to crown Him again,

King forever, ceasing never

over us all to reign.

Frankincense to offer have I;

incense owns a Deity nigh;

prayer and praising, all men raising,

worship Him, God on high.

Myrrh is mine; its bitter perfume

breathes a life of gathering gloom:

Sorr'wing, sighing, bleeding, dying,

sealed in the stone-cold tomb.

Glorious now behold Him arise,

King and God and Sacrifice;

alleluia, alleluia!

Earth to heav'n replies.

—JOHN H. HOPKINS, 1820–1891

ave you ever thought about what has happened because Christ came to the world? Our world has felt the mighty impact of Jesus Christ.

His COMPASSION has made the world more compassionate.

His HEALING TOUCH has made the world more humanitarian.

His SELFLESSNESS has made the world more unselfish.

His SACRIFICE has made the world more self-effacing.

Christ drew a rainbow of hope around the shoulders of men and women and gave them something to live for. If Christ had not come, this world would indeed be a hopeless world. If Christ had not come, this would be a lost world. There would be no access to God; there would be no forgiveness; there would be no Savior.

The wise men brought their gifts of gold, frankincense, and myrrh. What are you giving to Christ this Christmas? The gift He wants most is your heart. On that first Christmas God gave us His Son. What He wants from you is your surrender, your life.

—DECISION, December 1990, "The Night an Angel Spoke"

But You

It isn't your gold or silver,
your talents great or small,
your voice, or your gift of drawing,
or the crowd you go with at all;
it isn't your friends or pastimes,
your looks or your clothes so gay;
it isn't your home or family,
or even the things that you say;
it isn't your choice of amusements,
it isn't the life you lead,
it isn't the thing you prize the most,
or the books you like to read;
no, it isn't the things you have, dear,
or the things you like to do,
the Master is searching deeper . . .
He seeks not yours, but you.

—Ruth Bell Graham's Collected Poems

*Thanks be to God
for His
indescribable gift!*

—2 Corinthians 9:15 nkjv

I n a little town in Florida there was an unpretentious home for small, unwanted boys. Having little of this world's goods, the kindly matron made it up to them the best way she knew how. She loved them, mothered them, fed them, taught them to love God, to read their Bibles (those old enough to read, that is), to say their prayers. She laughed with them, listened sympathetically to their troubles (even while she stirred the soup), made her corrections few, her exhortations brief, and then she loved them some more.

One day—this is a true story—a well-to-do lady from a distant city came to see about adopting a boy. Everyone was pleased and happy for the fortunate little boy who was going to have such a fine home—such a successful man for a father and such a beautifully dressed lady for a mother.

The lady smiled down at the small boy and asked, "Do you have a bicycle?"

"No, ma'am."

"Well," she promised, "we will buy you one. And have you roller skates?"

"An old pair," he replied.

"We'll buy you a lovely new pair. And tell me, have you a transistor radio?"

The boy looked puzzled. "I haven't got any radio at all," he said.

"Well, never mind, we'll get you one."

Still puzzled, the small boy studied her solemnly—then blurted: "Please, ma'am, if that's all you're going to give me, I'd rather stay here."

This is the Christmas season—a time for giving and receiving gifts. So it has been, since the Wise Men brought their gold and frankincense and myrrh to the Christ child.

For weeks now, we've been shopping—shopping—shopping.

Perhaps skis for that strapping son, a negligee for mother, that heirloom bracelet for the daughter who has admired it for so long, a leather lounge chair for your husband, choice books, homemade fruitcake.

In this brief interlude before the final rush, let's pause and hear again the small boy's puzzled question:

"Is that all you're going to give—?"

"Is that all!" you ask. Your budget is knocked into a cocked hat already. "What do you mean—'Is that all!'"

Just that—"Is that all!"

I'm sure you remember the story of the hoodlums who broke into a department store one night; but it bears retelling. They didn't steal or destroy anything. They just had a wonderful time switching price tags. The next morning customers were puzzled and delighted to find fur coats selling for $5. Cold cream was priced at $150. A silver service was marked $1.75 and a pair of ladies' nylons $390. There were umbrellas for $1,000 and diamond rings for $2.

Has something come into our lives and switched the price tags? Are things of time of more value than things of eternity? Are material gifts worth more than gifts of the spirit?

Do we place high price tags on the community rather than on the family? On personal pleasures rather than the needs of those we love? On a television program rather than family prayers?

The Christian world remembers—however confusedly, however commercially—that this is the Advent season, a time for joyous giving.

But we have confused the real gifts with the material ones. We have our price tags mixed. What can we give, who have so little to offer? Ourselves.

Remember, that's what God loves so much. All He asks this Christmas is you. You, with your failures, your sins, your problems, your fears. *You.*

This is Christmas—the real meaning of it. God loving, searching, giving Himself—to us. Man needing, receiving, giving himself—to God.

Redemption's glorious exchange of gifts! Without which we cannot live; without which we cannot give to those we love anything of lasting value.

This is the meaning of Christmas.

—Ruth
Decision, December 1965, "This, Too, I Shall Give"

Because God's Son,
Jesus Christ,
has entered this world,
we know beyond a shadow of doubt
that joy and hope can be ours
if we will but receive the
gift of Christmas.

uppose you went to your mailbox tomorrow to find a very formal looking envelope with the seal of the British crown on it. I am sure you would open it excitedly to see what sort of royal greeting Her Majesty the Queen was sending to you. God, the King of Heaven, has sent you and me a message. What is that message? John 3:16: "For God so loved the world, that he gave his only begotten Son, that whosoever believeth in him should not perish, but have everlasting life." It speaks of a gift God has for us. It is the heart of the Christmas message.

This message tells us first that *God is the Giver of the gift.* We would expect God to give the ultimate in gifts, and He did. The Scripture says that He "spared not his own Son, but delivered him up for us all . . ." (Romans 8:32). God gave a Person as a gift to every one of us, and that Person is Jesus Christ.

Second, the message tells us that *the motive of God's gift was love.* Christmas tells us that God loves us. He is a God of love.

Third, the message tells us that *the whole world is the receiver of God's greatest gift.* Most gifts are labeled for and given to certain individuals, but God plays no favorites; He has no pets. It is to the whole world of men and women with their longings, their disappointments, that He sends the supreme gift of His love.

Four, the message speaks of *the value of the gift.* Sacrificial gifts are the expression of genuine love. God generously, loving, and sacrificially gave His only Son as the atonement for our sins. It is impossible for us to estimate the value of the gift that God gave. This was His only Son, yet God gave Him gladly because He loved the world so much. Such is the glorious and wonderful generosity of God. It is beyond our comprehension.

Fifth, we find in this message *the personalization of God's gift.* My wife and I love to get Christmas cards. Each year we go through them one by one. The ones that impress us the most are the ones that have handwritten messages on them. They seem more personal.

When God made His gift to you and me, He made it personal. I am convinced that Christ would have died on the cross if I had been the only sinner in the world.

He would have given His life if you had been the only one in the world who needed redemption. God made His gift personal.

But a gift is not a gift unless it is accepted. God does not force His gift on us, but He asks us to receive by faith the gift of His Son, Jesus Christ. It is my prayer this Christmas that you will reach out the hand of faith to receive the gift that Christmas celebrates.

—DECISION, DECEMBER 1973, "GOD'S GREATEST GIFT"

O Come All Ye Faithful

O come, all ye faithful, Joyful and triumphant,
O come ye, O come ye, to Bethlehem.
Come and behold Him, Born the King of angels;

Refrain
O come, let us adore Him,
O come, let us adore Him,
O come, let us adore Him,
Christ the Lord.

Sing, choirs of angels, Sing in exultation;
Sing, all ye citizens of heaven above!
Glory to God, In the highest; *(Chorus)*

Yea, Lord, we greet Thee, Born this happy morning;
Jesus, to Thee be glory given;
Word of the Father, Now in flesh appearing. *(Chorus)*

—John Francis Wade 1743

A Night *of*
Everlasting Love

The God of the
universe came from Heaven
and took human form.

ometimes in the rush of Christmas activity we forget that the most wondrous part of Christmas is the incarnation—the fact that in the person of Jesus Christ, God became flesh in order to save us from our sins. The great mystery of the incarnation is the crux and the core of the Christian message.

The prophets wrote of it, the psalmists sang of it, the apostles rejoiced and built their hopes on it, and the Epistles are filled with it. Christ's coming in the flesh— His invading the world, His identifying Himself with sinful men and women— is the most significant fact of history. All of humanity's puny accomplishments pale into nothingness when compared to it.

Isaiah said, "Behold, a virgin shall conceive, and bear a Son, and shall call His name Immanuel" (Isaiah 7:14). The Savior's entrance into the world was mysterious, beyond the grasp of the rational, natural person. But as God in the person of Jesus Christ walked and talked with people, they were conscious of the fact that God had manifested Himself in the flesh. Hearts that had been repelled by empty forms of religion ran to Him as starving men and women to a feast.

The distant heavens and the remote earth, the elusive God and the wayward human, were brought close to each other. Men and women, fettered and bound, were incapable of coming to God, so God in love and mercy came down to earth to interact with humans. Wonder of wonders! God incarnate! God clothed in a human body in the person of Jesus Christ.

The doctrine of the incarnation means that God came right down amid the sin and confusion of this world. It means that God was capable of participating in our pain, our suffering, our conflicts, and our sorrows. It proves to us that His love was not just a vague theory sung in ancient sonnets or proclaimed by shepherd mystics of the backcountry. It was real, vibrant, and realizable.

He came to the world, once and for all, that we might forever know that He has an absorbing interest in the way we live, the way we believe, and the way we die. He came to demonstrate to us that God and mankind belong together.

On that first Christmas night in Bethlehem, "God was manifest in the flesh"

(1 Timothy 3:16). This manifestation was in the person of Jesus Christ.

What an incredible truth! Think of it: The God of the universe came down from Heaven that first Christmas night and took human form! As the words of the familiar Christmas carol declare, "Veiled in flesh the Godhead see; hail th' incarnate Deity." The Scripture says concerning Christ, "In Him dwells all the fullness of the Godhead bodily."

This manifestation of God is by far the most complete revelation God ever gave to the world. If you want to know what God is like, then take a long look at Jesus Christ—because He was God in human flesh. In Him were displayed not only the perfections that had been exhibited in the creation—such as wisdom, power, and majesty—but also such perfections as justice, mercy, grace, and love. "The Word was God. . . . And the Word was made flesh and dwelt among us" (John 1:1, 14).

To His disciples Jesus said, "You believe in God, believe also in Me" (John 14:1). This sequence of faith is inevitable. If we believe in what God made and what God said, we will believe in the One whom God sent.

—DECISION, December, 2006, "The Mystery of the Incarnation"

LESS AND MORE

There will be less someday—
much less,
and there will be More:
less to distract
and amuse;
More, to adore;
less to burden
and confuse;
More, to undo
the cluttering of centuries,
that we might view
again, That which star
and angels
pointed to;
we shall be poorer—
and richer;
stripped—and free:
for always there will be a Gift,
always
a Tree!

—RUTH BELL GRAHAM'S COLLECTED POEMS

Christ has given
unsparingly of Himself,
His healing,
His compassion,
His love,
His understanding,
His power,
His wisdom,
and His redemption.

used to wonder why God did not send his Son full-grown, why God made Jesus to be born of a woman. Jesus had to go through childhood. He had to grow to be a man so that He could fully be one with us. He walked where each of us has to walk every day. He lived where each of us has to live every day. He lived with us so that He might set an example; He went through life so we might follow in His steps. God chose to dwell among us.

The Lord Jesus Christ came to rejoice with us. He came to share the sorrow and the burdens and the hurts that weigh us down. When God demonstrated that the "Word dwelt among us," (John 1:14) he was actually saying to you and to me, "My name is Emmanuel. I want to live with you. I will not live in isolation from you. I will not abandon you. I will not leave you comfortless (see John 14:18). I will love you with an everlasting love (see Jeremiah 31:3). I will stand with you—guiding, strengthening and comforting. And my proof is the sign of a Baby born in Bethlehem and of a Savior dying on the cross and rising from the grave." How wonderful to know that Christ can dwell in our hearts by faith right now.

When God said that He came to dwell with us and in us, He meant that He came to share every experience in our lives (John 14:17). When we cry, He weeps with us. When we agonize, He struggles too. When our hearts tear in disappointment, His heart breaks too. When we suffer pain, His heart is broken too. When we rejoice in happiness, He rejoices too. He lives our lives with us.

How wonderful that the mighty God of heaven completely identifies with us! This is how real and how close God is right now to us.

The meaning of Christmas is that God has come in Christ His Son to redeem each one of us who will believe in Him. He came to live among us—to take our humanity and to understand our needs, to set for us an example of love and obedience.

God dwelt among us to die for us, to be raised again. He is alive and gives to us the hope of the coming again of the Lord Jesus Christ. Jesus lived and died and rose again because He loves each one of us.

This Christmas season I ask you, Is Christ real to you? Does He actually live in your heart? Has he taken up residence in your life? Let Him be born in your heart today.

—DECISION, December 1979, "Does God Fit Into Christmas?"

et me offer for our consideration a revised shopping list—

This Christmas I am giving my **parents** more loving appreciation for the years of time and effort—yes, and money— that they invested in me, so much of which I took for granted.

To my **neighbors**—nice or not—I will give thoughtful consideration. I will be slow to gossip, quick to sympathize, ready to help—praying all the while that God will give them the necessary patience to live next to me.

To **those who serve me in restaurants or shops**—grumpy or obliging, taciturn or otherwise—I will be courteous, friendly, interested, remembering: If I worked so long for so little, if my back ached and my feet hurt, and if when I got home I still had supper to prepare, I too would be grumpy, taciturn, or otherwise.

To **all I meet**—remembering that each carries burdens known only to himself, and some too big to cope with—I will say the kind things I want (but hesitate) to say.

I will tell them the nice things I've heard about them. I will express my appreciation warmly. If there's nothing nice to say—I'll do more than keep my mouth shut sweetly, I'll find something nice to say.

To my **husband**—remembering how much he has had to put up with and for how long—I will give a frank, honest reappraisal of myself. I will remember that happy marriages don't just happen. They are the result of good hard work. Then I will take my Bible and reread those timeworn, ageless passages that speak of love and marriage and the responsibilities and privileges of wives. Sensible, delightful, down-to-earth passages, which if any woman would follow would make her husband the happiest, most contented man on earth.

To my **children**—this Christmas I will be more articulate in my love and my appreciation of them as persons. If I cannot give them a perfect mother I can at least give them more of the one they've got—and make that one more loving. I will be available, knowing that a mother needs, like God, to be "a very present help in trouble." I will take time to listen, time to play. Time to counsel and encourage. In a world of confusion and uncertainties, I will give them the eternal verities of the Word of God. I will try to help them cast their anchor on the goodness and mercy of God.

This is my revised list for Christmas. And through this type of giving, grows the giver.

—RUTH
Decision, December 1965, "This, Too, I Shall Give"

*Christmas is
just the beginning.
It will go on forever
and ever.*

—Eugenia Price

hristmas was the day when God ensured forever that nobody need ever be lonely again. One of the most honored names of Jesus Christ is "Immanuel," and the word "Immanuel" means "God with us."

Just as those first shepherds heard the celestial music echoing over the countryside, and the Magi from the east discerned that a strange new star had come into their universe, so thousands today are hearing by faith the distant melodies of heaven and are remembering once again the true meaning of Christmas.

On that first Christmas night, when the shepherds went to pay homage to the little baby in Bethlehem's manger, the angels were singing in the heavens, "Glory to God in the highest." Here was Jesus, not just a son of God, but *the* Son of God, ancient as the everlasting ages, yet young as a newborn infant, in eternity without mother, in time without father, conceived of the Holy Spirit.

That first Christmas, when in a drafty cave a newborn infant lay nestled in the straw, a pondering virgin was gazing into the face of Deity. Scarcely could the mother know that within those swaddling clothes was the one in whom were hidden "all the treasures of wisdom and knowledge" (Colossians 2:3).

The wise men of the day came to salute Him; and today we do well to pause and realize that in Christ is the wisdom for the solution of all our problems. As the wise men beheld, they could see the tiny, clenched hands of the baby boy which, some thirty years later, were to be ruthlessly wrenched open and nailed to a Roman cross for the guilt of the world; hands that were too small to reach up and touch the noses of the cows, yet would one day reach out to the multitudes, unstop deaf ears, open blind eyes, raise up the dead. Here was the one who had flung the worlds into space and lighted the sun.

Here were eyes as yet unable to follow the swishing tails or swaying heads of the beasts of burden, but they were later to look upon the masses and see that "the fields are white unto harvest."

Here were a little child's feet not yet able to sustain upright the one who strides through the corridors of the centuries, shedding light into dark hearts, leveling the rough places, straightening the crooked, erasing our sorrows, multiplying our joys and cleansing us from sin.

At this Christmas season Jesus Christ can make all the difference in the world in your home and in your life. Those who have truly caught a vision of the Christ of Christmas have become possessed by a spirit of high purpose. I am convinced that Christ alone is, as He said, "the way and the truth and the life"—for our nations, for our homes and for our personal lives. He is the source of spiritual fortification.

In Charles Wesley's hymn the idea of Christmas is clearly expressed:

Mild he lays his glory by,
Born that man no more may die,
Born to raise the sons of earth,
Born to give them second birth.

Jesus Christ can come into your heart at this wonderful season of the year, fill the aching void, forgive your sins, transform your life and make you a new person.

—Decision, December 1966, "Lord of Christmas"

Hark! the herald angels sing,
Glory to the new-born King,
Peace on earth and mercy mild,
God and sinner reconcil'ed.
Joyful, all ye nations, rise,
Join the triumph of the skies;
With the angelic host proclaim,
"Christ is born in Bethlehem".

Chorus

Hark! the herald angels sing,
"Glory to the new-born King".

Christ by highest heaven ador'ed,
Christ, the everlasting Lord!
Late in time behold Him come,
Offspring of a Virgin's womb.
Veiled in flesh the God-head see,

Hail the incarnate Deity!
Pleased as man with men to appear,
Jesus our Immanuel here.

Hail the Heaven-born Prince of Peace!
Hail the Sun of righteousness!
Light and life to all He brings,
Risen with healing in His wings.
Mild He lays His glory by,
Born that man no more may die,
Born to raise the sons of earth,
Born to give them second birth.

CHORUS

—CHARLES WESLEY, 1739

For God so loved the world
that He gave His only begotten Son,
that whoever believes in Him
should not perish but have everlasting life.
For God did not send His son into the world
to condemn the world,
but that the world through Him
might be saved.

—John 3:16–17 nkjv

esus came into the world to save all kinds of people: rich or poor, black or white, educated or illiterate, sophisticated or ordinary— or anyone in between.

Only two groups of people gathered at God's invitation to pay Him homage when He was born. One was the shepherds—lowly, at the bottom of the social ladder, uneducated, unsophisticated. The other was the wise men—intellectuals, from another race and country, wealthy, respected. The two groups could hardly have been more different!

God brought both groups to Bethlehem—one by an angelic announcement, one by the appearance of a miraculous star. And by bringing both, God was telling us that Jesus is the Savior for everyone. Every person stands in need of His forgiveness and new life—and every person can know it, if he or she only repents and makes that journey to the Christ of Christmas.

No matter who you are in the eyes of others, you need Christ. And no matter what you have done, He loves you and stands ready to welcome you.

His life began in the midst of persecution and peril. He came on a mission of love and mercy, sent by the Father. An angel announced His conception and gave Him His name. The heavenly host sang a glorious anthem at His birth. By the extraordinary star, the very heavens indicated His coming. He was the most illustrious child ever born—the holy child of Mary, the divine Son of God.

Yet no sooner did He enter our world than Herod decreed His death and labored to accomplish it. Warned of God in a dream, Joseph fled Bethlehem at night, taking Mary and the baby Jesus to Egypt until Herod's death finally made it safe to return.

As the "suffering Servant" He assumed a role of deep abasement. The Son of the eternal Father, He entered time and was made in the likeness of man. He assumed our human nature with all its infirmities, and weakness, and capacity for suffering. He came as a child of the poorest parents. His entire life was one long pathway of humiliation.

Now He is in Heaven, no longer limited by time and space. And some day He will come again—this time in glory—to take us to Himself. Are you ready for that day when you will meet Him face to face? Make sure this Christmas of your salvation, by repenting of your sins and asking Christ to come into your life and be your Savior and Lord forever.

—Hope for Each Day

Joy to the world! The Lord is come!
Let earth receive her King;
let ev'ry heart prepare Him room,
and heav'n and nature sing.

Joy to the earth the Savior reigns.
Let men their songs employ,
while fields and floods, rocks, hills and plains
repeat the sounding joy.

No more let sins and sorrows grow,
nor thorns infest the ground;
He comes to make His blessings flow
far as the curse is found.

He rules the world with truth and grace,
and makes the nations prove
the glories of His righteousness
and wonders of His love.

—Isaac Watts, 1674–1748

Every person
stands in need of
God's forgiveness
and love.

It's your heart
that Jesus longs for;
your will to be made His own,
with self on the cross forever,
and Jesus alone on the throne.

—Ruth Bell Graham's Collected Poems

Silent night! Holy night!
Son of God, love's pure light
radiant beams from Thy holy face
with the dawn of redeeming grace—

Jesus, Lord at Thy birth.

A C K N O W L E D G E M E N T S

Grateful acknowledgment is made to the following publishers for permission to reprint this copyrighted material.

Ruth Bell Graham, *Collected Poems* (Nashville: Thomas Nelson, Inc., 1977, 1992, 1997, 2007).

Ruth Bell Graham, *Our Christmas Story* (Minneapolis, World Wide Publications, 1959).

Billy Graham, *Hope for Each Day* (Nashville: Thomas Nelson, Inc. 2002)

Decision, December 1985, "The Event that Set Heaven Singing"

Decision , December 1986, "Responses to the Christ Child"

Decision , December 2001, "The Meaning of Christmas"

Decision , December 1968, "Good Tidings of Great Joy"

Decision , December 2000, "Are You Going to Miss Christmas?"

Decision , December 1962, "No Room in the Inn"

Decision , December 1988, "Immanuel! God with Us!"

Decision , December 1971, "The Night of Nights"

Decision, December 1987, "Christ, the Center of Christmas"

Decision, December 1989, "When God's Son Came to Earth"

Decision, December 1998, "The Message of Christmas"

Decision, December 2003, "Light for a Darkened World"

Decision, December 1980, "What Does Christmas Mean?"

Decision, December 1990, "The Night an Angel Spoke"

Decision, December 1976, "That Night Near Bethlehem"

Decision, December 1984, "The Peace of Christmas"

Decision, December 2002, "Unto You Is Born this Day"

Decision, December 2005, "You Can Know the Christ of Christmas"

Decision, December 1993, "Christmas a Time of Renewed Hope"

Decision, December 1969 "Christmas: God with Us"

Decision, December 1968, "The Quiet Corner"

Decision, December 1964, "The Light of the Star"

Decision, December 1999, "The Baby, the King"

Decision, December 1992, "The King Is Born"

Decision, December 1990, "The Night an Angel Spoke"

Decision, December 1965, "This, Too, I Shall Give"

Decision, December 1973, "God's Greatest Gift"

Decision, December, 2006, "The Mystery of the Incarnation"

Decision, December 1979, "Does God Fit Into Christmas?"

Decision, December 1966, "Lord of Christmas"